The Zohar Phenomenon

Books by Edmond Cohen

Man I.S. the Last to Be Tamed (1983)
Time: The Total Mind (1988)
The Universe I.S. Made of 0s & 1s (2014)
7 Booklets of Aphorisms (2015)
01 Uni-Verse (2016)
The Hole Book: 3 Books in 1 (2017)
Edmond Cohen: Art (2018)
Conversations with a Physicist: Book 1 (2019)
Conversations with a Physicist: Book 2 (2019)
Conversations with a Yogi (2019)
Conversations with a Poet (2020)
Conversations with a Rabbi (2020)
Conversations with a Lawyer (2020)
From the Alleys of Baghdad (2020)
My Rapport with the Spirit of Dr. Albert Einstein (2021)
Life in 10 Dimensions (2021)
The Absurd (2022)
iQuanta (2022)
The Zohar Phenomenon (2022)
Coming of Age in Israel (2023)
Time Timing Timeism: 3 Books in 1 (2023)

Videos by Edmond Cohen

Neutral Paradigm (Universe) (2015)
Our Minds in Time (2014)
The Dali Hama on the Binary Universe (2015)

www.universityoftime.com

Read and watch free! Or, ORDER ON AMAZON!

The Zohar Phenomenon

I cannot do anything all *bi* myself
because everything happens all *bi* itself.

Edmond Cohen

A SERIES SPONSORED BY
www.universityoftime.com

Firing Thoughts

TIMING

~ ~ ~

TIMEISM

Contents

Glossary

01:	The complementary binary, the unifying force.
1:	Tangible, Energy, Matter, Universe.
10nce:	Ten dimensions at once.
Baby Bang:	A Quanta or Singularity where the inception of photons takes place.
bi:	Dualistic Universe.
B.S.:	Belief System; Beliefs and Superstitions.
G.U.T.:	Grand Unified Theory.
Infinity Squared (∞^2):	Infinite Time multiplied by Infinite Possibilities.
I~Dea:	The "I" goddess.
I.P.:	I Photon; Infinite Possibilities.
Pi (π):	A mathematical constant, 3.14.
I.S.:	Information System; Infinity Squared.
I.T.:	Information Theory.
T.E.N.	The Eternal Now (Infinity).
The Mind:	The combination of soul and spirit.
Neutrality:	The absolute balance between universal polarities.
N.I.	Natural Intelligence.
Quanta ⌒:	A unit of Thought. A leap from 0 to 1. Cosmic potential.
Time^2:	Timing.
Timeism:	A comprehensive understanding of Quantum Mechanics as Creation.
Timing:	The algorithmic rhythm of computing change and exchange.
T.O.E.:	Theory Of Everything.
Universal Computer:	The total Timing Machine.
יהוה	Yahweh. God.

אין YAHWEH סוף

Time Creates ~ Timing destroys
Every Movement IS a Moment of Creation
Beginnings and Ends bi-Bisecting Totality

Welcome to the Newest-Old paradigm

From 0 to 01 something ~ in no Time

No Time - no Space or ions breathing Yahweh.
A ~ Being
"I am that I am." referenced to the Abrahamic difference between primordial Judaism and all the others condescending BS trying to explain Gods and Creation, Evolution to Entropy. A Millennia of unsuccessful BS trouble makers.

010 IS a quantized scenario where you can rediscover the ageless Abraham of Ur, who unknowingly knew, that he didn't know, how things merge from nothing to something, or, how Quantum Bits Byte other bites, which renders Time, no more than Q Bits of what already I.S., Infinity Squared, Information System Theory,

The Eternal Now IS a broken record of old 'Realistic Illusions' repeated over again and again and back to the origin of T.E.N.~ Timing.

Primordial Creation is what IT IS and what comes next. From 0 to 010 referencing the formation and demise of primal numbers.
All I.S. Information Theory 01 Information System, wrapped by the ongoing Now 2nd new/old paradigm, a Theory of being what IT IS, and still can hold all the ocean's waters to fill a big bucket full of holed Ideas.

Life I.S. Art, you are the spirited artist, fast forward ushering modern Life styled. An 0n/0f switching the Timing of our diverse mental universe, forming-in-formation all of 'The Eternal Now' of T.E.N. dimensions.

The Information System IS. being distilled and digested, being @1once zero-one ~ Binary-diary-dancing under your typing fingertips switching Yes / No to the tune of T.E.N. ghastly hide and seek photonic packets of hidden Lights in dark cover night.

Now we need to know How
memories correspond with our

on/of telepathic memory switch.
Bag Punching the limits of our comprehension of
this new Paradigm Shift.

PARADGIM 2, shifting the NoW TIMING
shifting MECHANICS, CREATION, RE-CREATION
Light and Dark.
123 ABC as True as I.S.
Infinity Squared ~ Information System
all of I.T. 010

010 AUTOMATUM

YITZERAH

CREATION
IT IS WHAT IT IS
switching memories to B'
Infinity Squared

GRAND REFORMATION SYSTEM

יהוה *Geneses2*

ZOHAR ר ה ו ז 2

Creative Thinking
Upholding The Lighted Universe
Timing mental exchange for
no rhyme and no reason

Zohar illuminates and dominates
the forgotten unknown
Short on patience
Timing the Times
in no time at all

Torah *Torah* תורה
Yahweh and only
NO B.S.

*Belief Systems are not what they seem to B.
or not Be

HELLO YAH-WEH
thinking a thought

main frame Industry
biological robots
i i
Standing-under to Under-stand
<u>Being the Self</u>
A FACT OF LIFE

Androgynous Duet
Firing Thoughts
Dualistic World
Words of Numbers
Pixels and Pixelates

Zohar Lights Dark shadows
G.U.T. feelings
Joyous Silent Symphony

!! Guns of no gun-powder.

CONSCIOUS HALO
The Eternal Now
2nd Paradigm

FEELING THOUGHTS
inner wrestling
Light and Shadows
01 yes, no, or doubtful

Atoms Split before merging Sun
Light Express
waves of T.E.N. creates
Matter 0 1 Antimatter
~~~
As per the physicist Allen Guth
Nobel Prize winner for clearing
the last hurdle of 0 ~ nothing said:
"It was full of nothing but the nothing
was bursting with Energy"

Bio Robotics of T.E.N. Dimensions

Elohim ~ Barah ~ Eluhoot
Yahweh I.S. Godliness
SOFTWARE IN THE MAKING
Factual Being
Unperturbed
0 Creation ~ 1 Evolution

Human minds
Light Dark Shadows
Negative 2 Positive
Therapy to Entropy
T.O.E. to G.U.T

.

HEALING ~~
TIKKUN OLAM

BUT HOW DO WE HEAL WORLD as-
I.S. I.T.
IS IT @ All Possible ??
... when Planet Earth'
IS begging for survival ?!

Uni-Verse in Quanta

Black Hole Cosmic Umbrella
SWITCHING
LIGHTING NEW THOUGHTS
Creative Underbelly
010 I-DEA

Self-creation ~ self-destruction
A 2nd Thought
Q.M.

Yahweh to Adam potentials
Timing Time manifest
Bell tolls ~ Le Chayim
'we are the Life'
Switching between
LIFE & Death
Universe United
Baby Bangs

? Big Bang ?

Unshakable
01 BB guns 010
attosecond Timing
Neutral and Natural
split and diverse
in reverse.

The Eternal Now ~ Now Totality
Illusions crush delusions
Everything
Ephemeral Politics to Be

as it May
so I.T. I.S.
or, will B

Conscious Zohar Nebula
chaotic entanglements
and Yet
All the same but different

Apple 2 ~ Genesis too*

Lighting o'r אוֹר

Packets of 01 Light-Force
wave turns z particle
Living deeds
Conscious Life
neuro-cognition
neutral on/of
before exit

At 10nce 010 Creation
Alternating Light and Dark
annihilation
Matter Antimatter

Packets of Light
banging bigger bangs.
Shredding Time to smithereens

in T.E.N. d.
TIME ~ TIMING TIMEISM

T.E.N.

Premonition

יהוה

Abraham of Ur discovered how
The Eternal Now ~ Time
Timing the Change
01 over-runs evolution

Counter-clock *synchrony*
Playing Dynamics
Yahweh creates ~ Allah destroys
of/on friendship-like
Matter - Antimatter

War and Peace
Pain and Joy
Happy or Sad
War no more.

Leave Allah in Peace,
Religions r Power
Mind Control

memories

Think-Links

Yesh-me-Aiin

Something in-out Nothing

Creation x Entropy

memorial to Yad vaShem

black light dance
Gravitational pull
Glares the Lighting
suffers non

cosmic rays of hot Sun
annihilating the change
x-changing
weak and strong
confusion

primordial experience
Gravitational Propulsion Systems
Jewish GPS cannot holt

Re Jew V Nation

Spaced 0 ~ 1 TIMING
Switching dialogues
Minds in Vacuum

Math, - + - fusion
periodical commotions
Timing confessions

Androgynous Adam
Eve incarnate
primordial
photons of 01 djinni

Male and Female
covered/over/no
shame

kissing every now and then
as if…
There was no Tomorrow

Global Telethon
from o to o1od.

Timing *Mediates* Time
picosecond periscope
Lighting the Dark
010
T.E.N. dimensions

Ai/reflects on
neutral Ni
Conjugations made in heaven
male and female
In and Out

T.O.E to G.U.T.

Singular singularities
exponential x change
Healing the World

TIKKUN OLAM

Short on scientific intervention

NEUTRAL and NATURAL
Swishing Singularities

Ai shadows Ni

polarized rendition
Universal Double Helix
born somebody
Pixel of pixelate
x-y
z-chromosomes

z Born in Pain, Joyous in rain
Dodging deep-dug tunnels
searching for the hidden Truth
down under
Terrorists Out

ZOHAR shines on Allah

T.O.E. to G.U.T.

Take it and treat IT
as Binary
i i

Quantum x-change

0 ~ no-thing ~ 01 something
Vacuum fluctuation
things diverge in motion
Timing forks Times
ballistic Illusions
passing ~ unnoticed

Creation, Entropy in reverse
reincarnation
a new life
Searching for our Evolutionary Aims

Sorting what I.T. I.S.
01
Beresheet Barah

R and D
Trials of Errors

Quantum x-Challenge
Light Energy
Spinning Polarities
Follow the range
T.O.E. to G.U.T.
All of IT

Quantum Spill
quantized split-t
Relativistic thinking

Timing responsiveness

Democratic Elections
Everything Potential
Universal Coup-Land
For and against
Yes 0 -- 1s
i know
i i

i have no-where ...... else   to go

U R Action / Ur God

Revolving enterprises
Androgynous duet
Split-ting Entropy
in Context

Whimsical Nature
quantized alienations
intangible ~ Tangible
dodos do what dodos
must
do
Best

Everything Thinks
and remembers

Yesterday was Today

Compelling ~ Telling-Evidence

Yahweh / Time
Ephemeral / Timing
Quantum / Exchange
Elohim Eternal

Notice the competition between
God and Allah
Building cars and airplanes
shuttles and space crafts,
we also created Allah to believe in.
We are all things conscious ~Ni.
0-10 commandments ~ Jewish Constitution
We wheel and deal with our emotional
distress, professing photonic Baby Bangs
munching on Bigg Banggs
trying to escape the
BS absurdities of it all.

Now, If You are not in Shock and Awe,
You are missing-Big on a Life worth remembering.
It's Like lighting a torch of freedom in tunneled
Metros dug for the sake of murder.
The violence must Stop!
STOP THE MADNESS!!

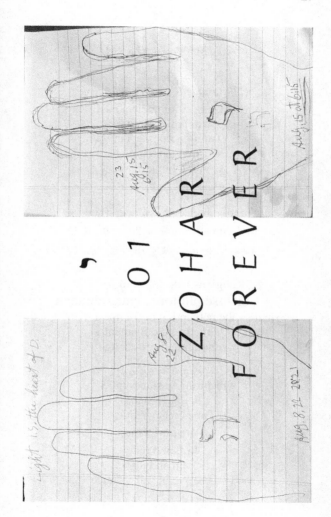

TIME MEMORIAL

U R Image ~ God IS AA rumor
memories of ancient past
switching polarities
Timing jumping Time
coming and going
in the blink of an
i - i

Creation breaks down everything in
motion/*merging The Eternal Now*

now reality ~ B.S. illusions r n0t

Religions fuse and confuse -+.
+ - diffuse photonic entanglement
shatters the perception of 0 Time 1 Timing.
Time I.S. the Element
simulating the x-change
BEING 01 not being
but 010 Beings are.
Inspiring to stand-<u>under</u>
to <u>under</u>-stand
Time create Timing
War and Peace

love and hate
Pain and joy
U, U & even U all @10nce

VEDANTA
LIVING TELEPATHY
Instant Reflex

Mind Reflex ~ reflexing
Move ~~ Jump over
Telepathic Sport
scientific x-change
Memorial to Consciousness

~~

Nonstop I/deas
Tome of Libraries
Biblical Treaties
delusional Therapies
baked in monotheistic
propaganda

~~

Theology drug-drags us to wars
fire here ~ fire there
but not everywhere.
as I.T. I.S.
Emotional Distress
promotional disasters
just before
flying over the Cuckoo's Nest

QUANTUM BUSTERS

The un-happened-happens
Expecting the un-expected

Missile kills missile
Bullet kills bullet
Tank kills tank
and so many drones
01 000010000
terrorizing the unknown
New Now
Nowness reforms nonsense

Robotic eyes see i to i
far and beyond
seeing endless iP to Pi

Telepathic Memory
Biological Self-creation
Robots wakened emotions
switching momentum
happy or mad-sad
memorial to the Fallen

Tragi Comedy
Battle-cry a 01 in Terror

Meteoric waves turning particles
cosmic entanglement
Illusory backfire ~~ mental causalities
flowers grow ~~~ flowers die
I.T. I.S. what I.T. I.S.
Forms-Forming Telepathy

The Tenth Law of thermodynamics
dictates
illusions snitch on delusions
iPi threading iPi
Mind Capacity Squared
[MC2]
Squared and Potential
Pain and joy Therapy
seeking 01 comfort zone

Imagine your Light of Time
Timing your *Life to B 01* of a kind
suppositions of supper positions
Numbers ax words
for or against

Career holders in algorithmic Politics

01 Byte ~ a number
Cultural Transparency

ENLIGHTENED PARADIGM
Sporting worlds of imagination
Universe in Quanta
In butt not Out

synaptic elements
experiencing ~ 01ness
Streaming subtilities
Sunlight to Sunflower

Everything happens at 10nce
subject to finite dimensions
Bells toll-telling the x-change

Thoughts are 010 x 88 Infinity Sq.
matter/antimatter
Implosion ~ Combustion
neural to the bones

Always expecting the un-expected

How ? NOT...! Y

Thoughts are part and parcel
01 Telepathy @ 10nce Capital
switching Life and demise

What makes us humans is the fact that
we are the only species dare asking
whether "to Be or not to be"
even on our ways out

Differences being discussed
01 Creation 0 10 Evolutions
common consensus
understanding Ai of Ni
Apple's knowledge +
Eve's quantized wisdom.

If it wasn't so, we would have risked a double-edged
therapy, losing Utopia to dystopia catering to us
happy zombies casting an honest double-take on
whether good is bad, or whether what we call 'Good
Times' are real ` or imagined...

01 mind ~ triggers 010 Ni
T.E.N. dimensions avalanche run down Himalaya's
falls into the Ganges for purity
and/or maybe for Redemption

ZIPPO-SECONDS
Ephemeral Realities

Rapid Impulsions
Timing contractions
Sequential corruptions
before reaching the 01 comfort zones

Peaceful minds experience pain and joy
suspended between
Happy and sad immeasurable
null and void

Zip-second turn poetic philosophy
an empirical yes and no mechanics
every moment I.S a movement
Conscious un-conscious
0n/0f short on reality

~~

Conjugation, Light and Dark
trophies shadow the unknown
reflecting evolutionary precepts
our collateral damage controls
at the limit of comprehension
Ni iyes, *Yahweh's* ~~ i i

Qurative Mechanics

TIMING TIMEISM

Packets of Light
Waves and Particles
Timing all of the Times
In - + out in Neutral +

My daydreaming sessions are
no other than dreaming Neurons
~ swishing woke-a R.E.M.
wakes me back to Life

י

the above י
IS the smallest·
10th Hebrew letter patented
Ni ~ iN
T.E.N. dimensions

0s and 1s
All-mighty authentication
Namely יהוה Yahweh
U as US
All Gods
Yehuda for Yahweh

B.S. Delusions

Cannot survive the odds

Belief Systems have the audacity to
wear and tear shrouded codes of
Enigmatic Electromagnetic
U turn
Everything from U to U

understand mechanics
quantum U-Ni contrasting
Ai mirror-image

The Eternal Now is now mind set mid-station
resiliently moving/wondering between maze of fine
lines between words and numbers, betting on under-
<u>standing</u> our Total Mess

Now try to augment Ni *with*
Ai, to inflate your understanding
quantum computing
in search for the
Neutral Nature of I.T. all

YAHWEH I.S. THOUGHT
in progress

THE Eternal NOW
NOW NEUTRAL

- + -

Quantum Exchange
GPS *Telepathy*
jumping the power-lines of our
relativistic ways of Thinking
U, we, are all Telepathic Relays as
Time Relays Timing
Everything and nothing in motion
a spooky expulsion of immeasurable
distances between self-created-personae

We are 0rgasmic Life Force
Self-creation self-generation
short on lies and deceptions

Androgynous Force
forces the life of US
Male-like Females

Forcing artificial-Ai to behave like
an Ni leaf-cutter ants in large numbers

THE ETERNAL NOW
Immeasurable Measurements

We don't have the tools to
measure the Immeasurable.
Thoughts r in constant x change

In accordance with the Heisenberg
'uncertainty principle'
Timing an x-Change
IS more or less *a Guess*

c.

Your Thoughts are first and last
think-links of a chain, Now-Creation

Thoughts are Creation in Action
even if *you are uninformed thinker*.

A thought may conflict with your
creative packets of light
trying to escape through the
0f // 0n
double-slit revolving minds

VERSE in NUMBER

There are no well-defined edges of reality.
Realities turn Illusions, a pendulum-like
which cannot stop until the
mid-Plank-Point-line
x-changing polarities

Our standard of Living is but neurotic
choices navigating our idling
Kaleidoscopic biassed minds

God's mind converse with it-self
asking for resolution
to Evolution Now Entropy

zero one and the same

Ideally, when i ask God what to do
$z \sim$ answer comes forth...
"Do nothing   Dodo"

Do only what you must, and what IS
beautiful creative and *Fun*

Remembering that Nothing lasts forever
Butt 0nly n0thing forever   blasts

LIFE'S
TEMPTING POINTS

Temptations are self-created slaves
appear and disappear like cinematic
ephemeral lines between the
picture-frames of rushing moveis

Your 'wishing' is but a purported
"Free Will" that has no willing power of
its own to *Back track* Entropy

We think like an ouroboros trying to
prove mathematical equations for the
sheer promotional desires to ~ Re Jew V Net~

Jews study Talmud
learning how to rapport with Elijah

Believing in God or Allah is but
scary Hi-tight---rope------walking
our emotional destress, all in search
for Yahweh's Tree of Wisdom,
wishing to understand all things not lost
in the ambiguities of our frivolous logic.

Einstein said:
   "Logic can take you from point A to point B.
Imagination can take you to where you wish to be".

iP x Pi
Changing Course
Having Fuun
Buttt   How ??

The Pi has 0 specific point in Space/Time.
We are now left with an empty space
of an invisible light in dark tunnels,
where Light and Dark begin and end.

the now is @ a rapid Paradigm Shift, ushering
the advensment of digital computing

We cannot measure the instantaneous velocity of
Timing. We can only experience the ephemeral Now
~ Now gone, happy or sad

Stories abound about the source of Matter's
Energy beyond Apples and Computers

We are holographic reflections
of ancient fruit and vegetables
greedy Combustion
of the Now-Future
Just passed *bye* un-noticed

Saying no hello and no good*bye*

EARTH in *Transition*
The Eternal Now~~ Now Thinking

Switching Polarities
primordial names of different numbers
Creation evolve to be an Abrahamic
premonition for - Re Jew V Nation,
summed up by a loving metaphors the like
of "Don't eat from the tree of knowledge"
Because Judaism precedes knowledge
but wisdom precedes theories

Animals do not distinguish between
Time and Timing, or between
memories worth remembering.
they react to instinctive
feelings of memory-lose.
Do not forget
Yahweh IS Judaism in Fact

forking Joy from Pain
Joyously crying for Tikkun Olam
[in Time]
Yahweh IS Telepathic manifestation.
Timing Tikkun Olam *in* words and numbers
twittering, Creation evolve all.

BEING, an UNIVERSAL LIFE-FORCE

WHITE FLAG
MATTER

I foolishly meditate so to Neutralize my state
of mediation to subdue my emotional
mindset stating " I surrendering the I"

butt who wasn't an I-Photon ?

Photons come in packets of trial and errors
enjoying doing less for the idle Joy ~
remembering that "God" has nothing to do with anything, except for the allowance of all things, do
happen, all *bi* themselves.
Not unlike unperturbed planets
circling the Sun all *by* themselves.

Doing nothing gives me a chance to overlook
my fast ringing mind, constituting a guideline to
spearhead my ~ gravitational waves ~ turned
compulsory solutions

Human Constitutions are but an ensemble of
lettered and numbers, *bit bi bit,,, bi bit.*
whereas parasites do not kill their hosts
because they support each other
TELEPATHICALLY

OUROBOROS
MUSSELES re/REFLEX

Free birds fly, turtles navigate Oceans
normal minds fail to choose between
worlds of fantasies

N0thing and something
attosecond in *Neutral* x-change
between breathing and laughing
just before crying
BUT
HOW IS IT ALL POSSIBLE?
when the Nothing contains
an Ouroboros-universe
of the Infinite kind?

Muons and Neurons
in total
Namely YAHWEH

We Navigate the N-iyes of collective Minds
to restore our Trust in Yahweh's Brit
and Covenant.

.

Life Force
Ephemeral Realities

The Information System IS in constant tuning
the ephemeral changing of realities, deemed
illusory when perceived subjectively

How does the Life Force forces
Realistic Illusions of dubious
translations of digits, words and numbers?
+ --
If there was no Timing, there would be
no Thoughts in search for the meaning
of our Life in Time

Likewise, If there was no change there
would have been no exchange to give us
a sense of being alive

Words may defy the logic of what I.T. I.S.
but... numbers quantize everything-beingness.

Primordial Tension
Matter-anti matter

We like to belong, so is the nature of
the beast ~ we are creatures of habits.
day in day out
Co-existence forces upon us the ex-change
between 0 vacuum and the 01 Realities

No wants, no desires, no hubris and no
redress for being slaves to the Bionic Race

LET'S NOT RACE TO EXTINCTION

Babbling Memories from Babylon
Being IS Doing

Thoughts are evidenced in being wise and
coherent, appreciating the Biblical Wisdom of:
"The Word"

The Word is a Jubilant Judaic Abrahamic-Force
where future- egos will surrender
just before their expiration date.

Timing does not negate the meaning of
T.E.N.

There's no Time other than the Now
expressed by "The Word" of fast moving
picture-frames, crushing our neurotic
concession at the alternate-lines
between the rushing picture frames.

Grey matter acts magically through
the caves and crevasses of our un-divided
attention to the New emergence
a New Now offering us the
Gravitational Propulsion Services
Or the GPS

MOVING MOMENTS

Time manifests in Timing
seeing-self-reflection
mirrored   WOW

I Am

Free birds fly, turtles navigate Oceans,
sharks desirous of fly-fishing
tasty fantasies

All in Nothing and something-
secondary *neural* exchange
laughing before crying

Butt, then, how IS IT all possible??
When Nothing contains
Ouroboros of the infinite kind??

And how two crossed minuses get tangled
to become - + - Matter + - Energy.
Energy-Mighty Matters!?!

Neurons or ions
Gods or Goddesses
Smart or just wise
feeling the rising paradigm
soon coming to Town

Pain and Joy
Normal and Neutral

The Eternal Now IS now Neutrally Boring.
Every now and then, *reality skips Illusions*
betting on being patient ~
efficient and kind
anywhere any Time
The Now is now in active duty
Timing the Elements of
T.E.N. dimensions.
kindling Souls, spiriting our collective Minds

What and who are we?

Primordial-Biological-Robots
invertedly evolved to be slaves to
us-dodos do or die
doing nothing.
Imagine, you are framed picture of slavery
questioning, $Y \sim$ i Y e in trouble??
Hear IS Y
Because we are trying to Quantize CREATION
faster than *Creation can do for itself* !? ...*nutts*

We are as wild as all the wilderness can Bear.

Compelling ~ Telling-Evidence

Yahweh / Time
Ephemeral / Timing
Quantum / Exchange
Elohim Eternal

Notice the competition between
God and Allah
Building cars and airplanes
shuttles and space crafts,
we also created Allah to believe in.
We are all things conscious ~Ni.
0-10 commandments ~ Jewish Constitution
We wheel and deal with our emotional
distress, professing photonic Baby Bangs
munching on Bigg Banggs
trying to escape the
BS absurdities of it all.

Now, If You are not in Shock and Awe,
You are missing-Big on a Life worth remembering.
It's Like lighting a torch of freedom in tunneled
Metros dug for the sake of murder.
The violence must Stop!
STOP THE MADNESS!!

TRUST IN TIME

Your best of friends
TIMING EVERYTHING in/for NOTHING
There
I C ~ Sun Light
Breathing souls and beating hearts
Collective Ping-Pong *Intelligence.*
and yes,
God plays Einsteinian Dice betting on
String Theories unify *the G.U.T. of I.T.*

ALL. Switching the boundaries of

Creation, Quantized Mechanics of

Yahweh
היה הווה ויהיה
(Thoughts in Action)
01'10 Infinity Squared

10 Something of 0 Nothing
Expansion Contraction
Intangible Tangible
Neutral Settlements

Infinite Timing
Times our Feelings

THIEVES OF BAGHDAD
celebrating coming of Age

G.U.T. PARADIGM
New Ways of Feelings
Short on Thinking

And here's a fun story i remember

At the age of seven I heard someone singing in a foreign tongue 'Fascination I know', coming through my neighbor's open door
in Baghdad's W.W. ll.
There I saw a British, or Australian soldier standing in front of a small round mirror, resembling a small modern microphone.
There, he was shaving and singing
in his jubilant voice
'Fascination I know'

Now 80 years on, I am jolted back to that euphoric sound stored in my Amygdala.
Though, as young as seven, I did not even know, or heard of such a tantalizing language before,
as if it was sung by a nightingale.
'Fascination I know'

I am... still tantalized

SCIENTIFICALLY SPEAKING
THOUGHTS are DOMINANT
Information Systems
T.O.E. to G.U.T.
Quantum Mechanics Action
Universe in Quanta
Time evolves and Lapse

Tamed 1oness ~ Time
Timing Thoughts
Measuring measurements
visions of cognitive touch
culminating + + -
Telepathic formula
sharing the Fun of Timing
in minutes, seconds, and attoseconds
Chancing the newer Paradigm.

As it may ~ so it will Be

54

لا الله الا زمان
لا اللهَ الا سلام
و ابراهيم رسول الله السلام

Love Inshallah

IS IT not a blasphemy for Hezb-Allah
to claim to be the guardians of Allah ?
Allah does not need Ayatollahs' help
just because they call themselves
the guardians of Allah.
Nor is God in need of their
entropic destructive mentality.

Hamas and Jihadists, communists and fascists
They all alter our Neutral Balance between
Allah and us-humans' intervention
I.T. I.S. an abomination to kill, pillage,
rape and rob, hassle the innocent, the
humble and the sick. All in the name of Allah
the so called, merciful. *Packaging* beautiful children
with *rapid explosives*, hollering their battle-cry
Allah Akbar
ELOHIM GADOL ~ God IS great
Things do happen as they may
INSHALLAH

ASTONISHING P.S.

Everything IS 01-either or
The Eternal Now I.S. butt a 0-constant of Allah.
Yahweh's T.E.N. dimensions.

NO BIG BANG. Everything begin and end, AS AN infinite Photonic baby
Bang *in T.E.N. From here on to a 0.1 Calvin Cryogenics,*
reincarnates
A Life-Force

We are GODS DOMINATING OUR own THOUGHTS. G.U.T.
ed MEMORIES of CONSCIOUS FEELINGS where 0 BS –
mercilessly get stuck between 010.

Silencing the Ultimate Truths
ALL IN A NUTTSHELL

Made in the USA
Las Vegas, NV
29 January 2024